AF486416

THE POWER TO CONTROL

HOW THE ELITE CONSPIRE AGAINST YOU

DECONSTRUCTING AMERICA PART 1

TOM S. PANE

Published with the assistance of Apathy Productions LLC

www.ThePowerToControl.com

https://twitter.com/Power2Control

FOREWORD

THIS book is the first part of a series entitled *Deconstructing America,* which attempts to explain, in a relatively easy-to-understand way, how the ultra-rich use their vast power and resources to manipulate the general population to support their beliefs and interests. The series will look at different aspects of how power is used to control people, all within the framework of the founding and development of the United States of America, to illustrate its arguments and support its conclusions.

I decided to write this series after being disappointed and frustrated by how little genuine, authentic information I could find on power and control. The info I was reading, watching, or listening to either had an agenda to begin with or was too academic and long-winded for most people to have the bandwidth to consume.

My goal with this pamphlet is to communicate progressive ideas that have been around for some time but have been absent from our social conversation for the past 100 years due to certain interests suppressing them from public discourse.

The ideas presented here are informed opinions, nothing more. Try not to get too offended if you hear things that you disagree with. It's OK. We don't need to convince each other that we are right or that we have all the answers all the time. What we need is an open and honest discussion about important topics and issues that affect us all.

I encourage people to question everything they see and hear from our business leaders and elected officials. Never assume someone who is in a position of authority knows better than you because they are in charge. As you will find as you go through life, those in charge typically have little mandate or rationale to be in such a position, so they will try to make you think they have something special going for them that a regular nobody, like you, could understand.

This book is about exchanging information and freedom of thought with no boundaries. It is not about pushing a particular ideology or point of view. It is about establishing an authentic discussion to achieve genuine results.

Without people possessing basic information about how those in charge gain and maintain control over individuals and the population at large, no one can have a productive discussion about how to address the issues we all face.

Do not let our leaders tell you what the topics of discussion are. It is essential that you set the stage, agenda, and conditions for debate yourself, and not allow others to force you into a loaded discussion designed to tilt the scales in their favor. If you let someone else set the stage for debate, let's say a corporate media company or a politician, they will rig the game to their benefit, so you can never win or even enter into the right talk to come to a reasonable solution.

Much of what I will discuss in these pages has been addressed by various free thinkers for decades. Still, these topics have been censored from mainstream corporate media and government communications throughout this century.

In terms of influences for this book, the person I align with the most politically and intellectually (in terms of ideas, he is much more intelligent than I am) is Noam Chomsky. Some of this pamphlet draws on and references Chomsky's ideas, which overlap with mine. Plus, he is a brilliant academic who conducted extensive, evidence-based research on power and control. If you want to delve deeper into independent and critical thought, check out the following books by him.

Understanding Power: The Indispensable Chomsky

Media Control: The Spectacular Achievements of Propaganda

Manufacturing Consent

Manufacturing Consent: The Movie

Another significant source I drew from, at least in relation to the founding of the United States of America and the forming of the U.S. Constitution, is *A People's History of the United States* by Howard Zinn. This book is an excellent supplement to all that history you learned in school, now told from the perspective of the millions of ordinary people who actually lived through history, in real life, rather than the manufactured storyline we learned in school.

We all need to understand how those in charge wield their power and keep us under control. We all need a basic understanding of how those in power have used the same methods to control people for thousands of years, and that nothing being done right now is unprecedented. Yes, the times have changed, and the methods of control have evolved and become harder to spot, but it's the same old story, told time and time again. It's time that story had a real ending, not just another rewrite for a new generation.

This is a pamphlet of common sense, and it is addressed to the inhabitants of America, every single one of them.

THROUGHOUT all of modern human history, a very small number of people have been at the top of society, while the majority have been at the bottom, regardless of the form of government, social system, or time in history.

The numbers we are talking about are estimates and fluctuate over time, but after we left hunter-gatherer-type activities and started farming, real inequality between people began to emerge. This was about 10,000 years ago, when agriculture enabled landowners to accumulate wealth and pass it on to their heirs. Around this time, too, people began to domesticate animals, which led to further concentration of wealth among landowners.

As society became more technologically advanced and wealth became more concentrated, individuals became less equal. The landowning families who had wealth were able to pass it down to their heirs and then use that inherited wealth to buy political power, extending their control over the societies they lived in, eventually assuming the role of societal owners.

This process perpetuates each family's domination over its respective society, as power shifts between family groups and allegiances over time, generation after generation, to the present day.

The abuse and misuse of the majority by the elite minority is the real struggle in modern human history.

The modern human struggle is not about sex, religion, race, ideology, or any of the common themes elites and their media companies and institutions claim it is, as they rile up the populace to garner support for whatever actions and goals will benefit their own interests.

The true battle is **class warfare** between the owners of society and everyone else, as the elites of societies across the world conspire against the masses by directing the systems and institutions they own and control to create an imbalanced playing field that benefits themselves at the expense of all others.

For the purposes of this pamphlet, what do we mean by the word elite and who are those people exactly? The answer is no one you have probably ever met. The elites, depending on the period in history they occupy, and who you consider elite (monarchs, billionaires, etc.), only represent about .01% - .05% of the population, while the bottom is everyone else. In America, when we hear about the 1%, that includes the millionaire lackey class (CEOs, media pundits, political leaders), below the billionaire owners who help manage things and keep everyone in line and doing what they are supposed to.

The elites are the owners of our society.

But wait a minute…weren't we all taught in history class about how the American Revolution and resulting U.S. Constitution were a great experiment in liberal democracy, in which the poor huddled masses were brought up from their lowly origins to be given an equal place at the table by the educated and privileged elite? Didn't this grand experiment in democracy create the middle class, and improve the standard of living and conditions for all people, as a rising tide lifted all boats into a post-feudal industrialized wonderland of justice and plenty?

This pamphlet will spend a good deal of time dealing with this assumption since this is the type of propaganda programming all of us have had indoctrinated into us since our birth, and a tale that has served the American elites' purposes very well for the last few hundred years.

For more information on inequality in America and how the American Revolution was the beginning of a system of economic disparity, check out the book Unequal Gains: American Growth and Inequality Since 1700 by economists Peter Lindert and Jeffrey Williamson. Their research found that Americans overall were financially better off before the Revolutionary War than after, and "enjoyed higher living standards than Britain – and America's income advantage today is no greater than it was 300 years ago."

They also found that in times of great upheaval, like during and after the Revolution, the Civil War, and the Great Depression, "income inequality among Americans rose steeply in two great waves – from 1774 to 1860 and from the 1970s to today – rising more than any other wealthy nation in the world."

It seems the liberation from Britain and the tyranny of King George did lead to great wealth and plenty for some Americans – the elitists who manufactured the American Revolution.

CONTENTS

IN the 18th and 19th centuries, all the old systems of social control that had been in place for hundreds, if not thousands, of years, began to fall apart. It turns out, as the masses and the poor get more educated, like reading books and stuff, and smart people called scientists find out why things like eclipses happen, the plausibility of a King or Queen being a God themselves became a difficult tale to believe for the majority of people. Well, people asked, if the ruler isn't God or a descendant of God or appointed by God, then why do they have absolute power over us and can do anything they want, living in obscene luxury, while everyone else suffers and dies in poverty?

In places like France, many of those monarchs were torn down by popular revolution and put to the guillotine for their crimes against humanity as the common man rose against their oppressors. In France, people took to the streets and stormed the French equivalent of the White House, dragging the rulers from their thrones in public humiliation.

It is important to note that the American Revolution did not start as a popular uprising like the one in France. But if the American Revolution was not a popular uprising, how did it occur, and why are we told in history class and by our own ruling elite that it was the common people who revolted against the British crown?

Why did ordinary people who were loyal to the British crown and almost universally opposed to independence at some point decide the monarchy was bad and choose to join the new American elite (which included the Founding Fathers) to overthrow the British monarchy, even though it was a crime and treason to do so?

To put it simply, certain small groups of mostly wealthy aristocrats and business leaders in the American Colonies decided that self-governance of the colonies was preferable to being managed from abroad by another wealthy group (the British monarchy and aristocracy). These new American elites, who included lawyers, business owners, aristocrats, and landowners, didn't like England taxing their goods without local representation, along with many other grievances, and wanted to own the country they lived in, not just manage it for someone else.

The elites in America knew they did not have the general population's support for their desire for revolution; the population as a whole was loyal British subjects and had no interest in, or saw no benefit in, something as drastic as revolution. Eventually, the new American elites realized they needed to give up some money and power to certain commoners to gain support for taking control of the colonies away from the old elites. This compromise was possible in the New World because the wealth of the new land was so extensive that aspiring American elites could give up some things to people below them and still maintain their luxurious lifestyle. This compromise, which shifted some control and money down the chain and into the pockets of a new middle class, helped create what we now know as the United States of America.

How did the American elite gain support for the revolution from the common American citizen? With a few brilliant pieces of propaganda, such as the

Declaration of Independence and the United States Constitution.

By convincing the American people that the fight against Britain was not just switching faraway rulers for ones more local, but a grand battle for freedom and equality with lots of flowery language to get ordinary people excited and amped up, the new American elite was able to change enough of the populace from loyal British subjects to a group of rabble-rousing revolutionaries.

The basic methods of control by which American elites rallied support for the American Revolution are still in place to this day, helping to mobilize the populace to die in profitable but unpopular wars, and were modernized and reinforced during World War 1 through an organization called the Creel Committee.

When you look at the Declaration of Independence and the US Constitution, one thing needs to be made clear that is incontrovertible. The documents themselves, for all their talk of freedom, equality, and justice, represented less than 15% of the population at the time. They did not represent African Americans (slaves), Native Americans (savages), Indentured Servants (white slaves), women (semi-humans), and non-land-owning whites (everyone else).

How can documents that are addressed to 'We the People of the United States' and talk about 'all men being equal' only represent less than 15% of them? Those are not documents of freedom and equality, but ones of elitism and exclusion.

Those revolutionary documents only represented one group –
white European landowning males. All the other people who
were left out were deliberately excluded, including women.
Those who were left out were not considered fully human or
capable and deserving of the same rights as white landowning
men.

For example, indentured servants were bought and sold like
slaves; they could not participate in juries, and since they were
propertyless, they could not vote. More than half of the
colonists who came to North America were servants (white
slaves). Many were poor homeless children rounded up by the
hundreds on the streets of English cities and sent to Virginia
into forced labor.

This is the untold truth of our early settlers. They were not all
brave men and women seeking religious freedom and
opportunity, but mostly the dregs of society, waste people they
were called, and shipping them to the new world (also
considered a wasteland) was part of the elites' two-pronged
plan in England. The plan was to reduce poverty in England
(by shipping poor people somewhere else…far, far away) and
to get rid of their social undesirables (criminals, the
unemployed, minorities, and homeless orphans) to the new
world to be used as free and expendable resources in colonial
business ventures. If those waste people died en route or
during their harsh and short life in the colonies, it was not a
problem for English aristocrats; there was plenty more free and
expendable labor where that came from.

The Continental Congress, which ran America during the
revolutionary period, was dominated by wealthy men
connected through business and family ties, just as our
Congress is today. Back then, to run for Governor in Maryland,

for example, you needed about 5,000 pounds of property (about $1 million today) to qualify. This excluded 90 percent of the population from holding office since they did not have that kind of wealth. In colonial America, rich people could buy their way out of military service, but the poor could not.

What parts of the US Constitution (and the later addition of the Bill of Rights) were an olive branch to the new emerging middle class, as the old aristocratic elites recognized they needed public support for their revolution to take power from the old British elites. They gave up some money and power to the new middle class (merchants, traders, artisans), and then created some nice religious propaganda for the poor to convince them why the new management would make them freer and have a better life (Common Sense).

But the poor weren't so easily controlled and motivated by the rich. It was easier to buy off the emerging middle class. They get nicer houses, live a better life, and get to boss people under them around. The poor, white servants, and black slaves weren't seeing any immediate benefit to the revolutionary proposal; they were being abused by the rich and powerful and everyone else, regardless of who was in charge…and always had been.

This begins the American tradition of using words like freedom, democracy, and justice to rally rank-and-file support for the policies of the elite.

Positive language, nice pamphlets, and rousing tavern speeches weren't enough to keep the entire population under control and ensure they wouldn't pose a threat to the emerging American aristocracy during the revolutionary period. Those in power were in constant fear of slave revolts, and even more, the idea that poor whites and indentured servants would join up with black slaves to take power and control from the white elite. To counter this, institutional and systemic racism was and is still an effective tool. If the elites in charge in America could pit poor whites and blacks against each other, they were no longer as much of a threat to the newly emerging order of elite white European control.

Now that the new American elite, whom the Founding Fathers were a part of (most were wealthy and had economic reasons to support a revolution), had the support of the class below them and had a message and philosophy to push on the poor (Godliness, freedom, equality, justice), they then created and enforced massive state-sponsored racist legislation and discrimination to separate poor whites and blacks to ensure there would be no threat to their emerging ruling class.

I set the stage here for the reader to take a look at the American Revolution through a new lens. Step back from all your programming and indoctrination, from everything your parents rammed into your head…everything schools and the government have told you about how we came to be and hit the reset button. Suspend your assumptions to be a free and independent thinker for just a few hours, and see below the surface what may be happening that doesn't quite line up with the tales we are told in school, work, and church.

This molding of history, in which a positive dramatic narrative is created to make us all feel good and special about where we live and how we came to be, is exactly how power is wielded and maintained through the ages. Just as in a movie, TV show, or advertising campaign, a cherry-picked, fictionalized storyline is developed and then repeated by credible authorities throughout history until it becomes an assumed fact. It becomes history, the tale of conquerors, not a factual retelling of the world at large.

History itself is propaganda.

In the end, after all the manipulation and storytelling and tipping of the scales, power is ultimately wielded from the end of a baton or the barrel of a rifle. But the power structure is maintained from generation to generation and throughout history by manipulating historical and current events to align with the goals and beliefs of the ruling elite. Many of the goals of elites include keeping people ignorant, subservient, and pliable, so they can be directed and applied when and where needed. Ordinary people need to be directed on which wars to fight, which taxes to pay, and which jobs they will be permitted to have by the owners of their society.

The introduction uses the founding of the United States of America as an example of how the elite wield power to control the population. Long-term control is primarily achieved through manipulating the narratives of historical events and molding social culture and individual belief systems to align with the goals and beliefs of the rich.

Legal documents like the US Constitution, beyond their more conventional applications, are used to enforce elitist systems of repression and control through legislation.

Let's step back for a minute and talk about the general tools of control and some basic examples of how they are used for particular, specific objectives.

The primary goal of people who want something from other people (sex, money, labor) is **control**. With control, everything else flows from it, making one's actions justifiable (I never forced them; they willingly agreed). If you want to have sex with someone who doesn't want to have sex with you, controlling them first makes it much easier, and you won't get arrested for sexual assault later (Jeffery Epstein). If you want to take someone's money or pay them low wages, they can't survive on (Walmart, Amazon), having control over them through legislation is great. Not only are you allowed to rip them off legally, but the state makes it morally and socially acceptable to do so.

Control is the name of the game for the elite, and having the power to execute that control is part of a self-perpetuating cycle that feeds on itself. The more power someone has, the more control they can exert over those around them. With more control, more power is gained, and greater control can be applied.

Control occurs at both the individual and group levels.

Let's start with the first thing that needs to be controlled – you, the individual. If you are pre-programmed from birth to think the way that elites and rich people want you to think, you probably won't get out of line somewhere down the road and cause them problems. Since the previous generation of elites programmed your parents, they will, in turn, program you with their values, and mixed in with the programming you will receive from school, work, church, and peers, will eventually become your belief system. Some people reject those belief systems, or think they do, but all our early programming is essentially hardwired into us, and some is nearly impossible to alter.

While you may think you are a free being, coming up with your own ideas and finding your own path, I hate to break it to you, but you are not. You have been programmed and set up for a predefined life script, carefully orchestrated to make you a productive member of society. This means you do the things rich people want you to do to make them money and increase their power and influence. If you don't do those things, you are a deviant, an outsider, and most likely a troublemaker. The individual is programmed by their parents, leaders, schools, and society as a whole to fit into whatever mold society's owners want them to fill. This programming is the first stage of control.

The first stage of control is called indoctrination.

You have heard of indoctrination before; perhaps it was in a company you joined that explained the corporate culture and how you need to fit in, and in fact, you will learn that fitting in matters much more than what you actually do or bring to the table. The company is indoctrinating you, telling you upfront what way of thinking and behaving is culturally acceptable in this particular organization. If you fall out of line, you will be reprimanded and then fired, regardless of how well you perform at your job. You have heard of this in religious cults, too. When people are brought into a cult like Scientology, they are told what the rules of behavior and conduct are, including proper ways to think and process information. If you fall out of sync with how the organization wants you to think and behave, you will be excommunicated.

The same premise holds across all societies, of all shapes and sizes. Using the United States of America as an example, we are indoctrinated into the way the elites in America want us to think, act, and behave by having their values programmed into us from birth by our parents, friends, teachers, church leaders, and other forms of authority. You are taught what values Americans are supposed to have (independence, competition, hard work), what things you are supposed to want (money, marriage, kids), and what goals and activities you will participate in that will be good for society overall (volunteering, military service). But falling out of line in society, the punishments are much harsher than falling out with a company. You will not be fired, first you will be warned, then made an outcast, and then imprisoned or worse for your thought crimes against the state.

Indoctrination is the key to maintaining control across generations and with very young people. Just like the Nazis did with the Hitler Youth, if you program children with a philosophy or mindset before they have been programmed with anything else, they will be a willing servant for life. You have less need to keep them in line later with violence if they believe hook-line-and-sinker in the fairy tales that have been pumped into them repeatedly since birth.

Indoctrination doesn't last forever if the real world doesn't line up with the tales that were spun to you as a child. Have you ever had that experience at some point in your life? When you realized that what your parents and teachers were telling you about something forbidden (drugs, sex) didn't line up with your real-world experiences. That is your brain questioning your indoctrination.

The next stage of control reinforces indoctrination with ongoing conditioning.

In places like the U.S., this is done primarily through corporate media outlets. Corporate media in America claims to be the voice of the American people. They claim to be a check on power. They claim to present unbiased news.

The reality is that the media espouses the viewpoints of the elite by creating content within a moral structure that serves the goals of the rich. This content is then distributed through various channels (FOX, MSNBC, NY Times, CNN, Washington Post) to alter public opinion, not to educate people on all sides of an issue. The message is so intertwined with their daily reporting that it becomes part of the background noise and not something anyone questions or even thinks to question.

For example, in the US, it is assumed that the critical topics of the day are the environment, taxes, abortion…you know the list. As a general rule of thumb, any issue you see in the media is not a real issue, but an extension of a genuine issue they don't want to talk about. The real problems are whatever they are not talking about and trying to distract you from.

For example, the climate crisis is not about private citizens changing their behavior and not using plastic straws; it's an issue of corporations that are running amok and profiting off the destruction of our world, and a government that is doing nothing to rein them in. The climate crisis is about corporatism, as corporate money has bought elections and politicians, who now set policy that reduces regulations to address global warming. The citizen has no seat at the table in addressing any issue, but they will be the ones to pay for them in the end.

How else are people controlled, and how are the lower classes controlled if they are not consuming tons of corporate media and getting money, positions, and resources to push the agenda of the billionaire elite like the upper middle classes?

Control is further applied through religion, alcohol and drugs, sports, and entertainment (movies, TV, video games).

Elites and their lackey henchmen (CEOs, political leaders, media pundits) want people to think that the only solution to their problems exists outside of elite influence and accountability. Their first method to divert accountability is to convince the ordinary person that if they see anything wrong in their personal situation, it is a character flaw they have (you're lazy, not motivated, not positive), and has nothing to do with the system around you (elites gaming the system to screw you). Or, other things outside elite control may be causing you issues, but those are supernatural issues that can't be solved here by ordinary people (people are just sinners; God has a plan). This is all aided by a commerce system that gets people doped up on alcohol and prescription opioids to keep them complacent, with a side benefit of driving some serious profit for the elites who own the drug companies (win-win) (The Sacklers).

Finally, elites want to keep people wrapped up in the never-ending world of sports and competition, taking up most of people's time (and money) outside of work and family (more win-win). Since elites own all the companies that produce all types of entertainment, they profit from their application of control.

Think about it. It used to cost money and reputation to keep people in line. You put out political propaganda, beat people up, and throw them in jail; that was the way old-school leaders kept their people in line. Now, people are controlled by the very same forces that enrich and strengthen elites – consumerism. Win-Win-Win.

Another method of control is the manipulation of language, which is used in the media, government, and organized religion to introduce words with dual or loaded meanings, benefiting those who set the conditions of debate. For example, in America, someone who is an illegal drug addict is a criminal who should be in prison. In contrast, an alcohol addict is an alcoholic who has a disease and needs medical help. Two people suffering from the same condition, one an outsider and criminal, the other a productive member of society who just needs a leg up.

All of the above methods are used to keep the general populace in line by never letting them think there is any way to get out of line. If you assume we are a democracy and a free nation, you never question them.

If the indoctrination, conditioning, religion, alcohol, drugs, and sports are not enough to keep your mouth shut, those in charge have more direct methods for gaining your control and support. First, they can excommunicate or blacklist you. You'll see this all the time in business or political circles. A particular reporter wrote a negative article about the War in Iraq, and after that, could not get a job with any corporate media outlet and was sidelined to a local paper for the rest of their career.

Next, if you keep being a thorn in the side of the elite, like let's say, Julian Assange, you just arrest them and turn the judicial branch on them. Throw them in jail and see if that changes their point of view. Finally, suppose those pesky independent thinkers continue to think and say things that are offensive to the elites. In that case, they will be killed, either extra-judicially (Khashoggi), or through the judicial system (The Rosenbergs).

The rich and powerful have endless methods and resources to apply this control. They control governments and war and can direct aggression wherever they want. They control printing and the media, and determine what information is disseminated to the public and how it reaches the public, creating cover stories and a rationale for their warmongering and profiteering. They control all business and all infrastructure.

Everything that makes the modern world tick is in the hands of a very small group of extremely wealthy families and individuals. They can shape whatever narrative they want (global warming isn't real), and put that narrative into government legislation (EPA), into fiction (entertainment), and into news (media). Through their ownership of corporate interests and overall control over government policy-making, the same message is being created and promoted at all levels of our society. None of this is being done in a democratic or public way in any fashion, as you are commonly told.

Does this sound like a democracy to you? What type of system does this sound like to you?

THE purpose of our public educational system, much like the purpose of the corporate media system, is not to educate and enlighten people to participate in a free democracy but to indoctrinate and condition them to fit into their prescribed role in American society.

I remember distinctly, as a kid going to public school (good ones in nice communities), that I did not feel any school I attended was educating me to think and reason. I always felt it was teaching me to remember things, follow rules, and compete with others in exams and in school (sports). This memory training, order-following, and competition with others don't really do much to build you into a dynamic person with complex thought patterns who may question those in authority and their right to govern. What it does do is make you a good, productive member of the business and religious community, who can remember directions and follow orders. And that is by design, not accident.

Religious groups originally set up schools in America to teach people to read the Bible and other religious texts and to socialize (indoctrinate) children into the proper and moral way (Christian) of living. It wasn't until the 19th century that all those one-room schools popped up, as you see in history books, and the goal of their creation was not to manufacture intelligent and informed citizens to participate in our democratic system. The goal of the institutionalized public educational system was to train and convert thousands of farm workers into factory workers. As our economy shifted from a feudal, farm-based system to an industrial one in the mid-19th century, the government (in the service of business interests) had to figure out how to train people to work in factories. So, they created the public school system to do that.

The public-school system's goal is to indoctrinate and condition American youth to be obedient and productive employees and consumers.

From public schools to elite universities, people from different social and economic classes are trained for the world they can expect in their particular social strata. Poor people in poor areas going to public schools get a specific type of education to prepare them for being at the bottom of society, as the working and middle class receive their own indoctrination in more upscale public schools. Finally, the wealthy can expect to send their kids to private schools or elite boarding schools. Those elite kids can expect to be admitted to Harvard or Yale, and their future as a leader of our society is all but guaranteed if they want it. Of course, you may have noticed that every vital job in our government and all the best jobs in the private sector are held by elite graduates of the top prep schools and universities. From the Supreme Court to top writers from your favorite sitcoms, elite Harvard graduates are groomed for a life of success and leadership.

According to research by Burke, Hall, and Katz, the nation's small colleges helped young men transition from rural work to urban jobs in the 19th century. In contrast, the more elite colleges became increasingly exclusive and focused on the offspring of wealthy families, helping institutions like Harvard contribute to the creation and maintenance of a new elite class in the Northeast, who continue to run our country today.

All of this class stratification through educational indoctrination is an effective tool for those in power who want to do a few essential things. First, they want to keep ordinary people separate and fighting against each other so they don't focus their time and attention on the elites. Second, people of all strata are indoctrinated in school to compete with each other through grades (I did better than you) and in sports (us against them; winning is everything). This competitive role-playing is reinforced later in life after people leave school and extends to all parts of American life. It can be in politics (Republicans vs. Democrats), in sports (Yankees vs. Red Sox), or in race (Black vs. White).

All this is done to distort the issues and divert attention from the actual battle. A 10,000-year-old struggle of class warfare…the elite rich against everyone else.

THERE are many lesser-known terms related to power and control used in academic literature. One such term is the public mind, as academics call it. This basically means how the public at large thinks and sees things, as a collection of individuals. The public mind, or more commonly, public opinion, is critical because that is what elites in power are trying to control when they put out PR and propaganda. They want to shift public opinion toward a desired goal or action. It can be making people angry (immigrants are taking your jobs!) or it can be making them scared (global warming will kill us next year!), or it can be to motivate them for a more targeted purpose (go to WAR!). Luckily, getting people angry and scared is pretty easy to do, and both states make people pliable to do things like go to war, increase police, censor things, persecute people, and throw undesirable types of people (like your political opponents) in jail.

Oh, you will hear lots of noble reasons why public opinion needs to be controlled. We know what's good for you since some people are more moral (religious), better educated (Harvard), or more mature (older) than others. Or, we need to protect people from themselves (making alcohol and drugs illegal) since they can't be trusted to make up their own minds. (Paternalism)

From the very beginning of our history, American elites believed that elite intellectuals should oversee the population to keep them in line and pointed in the right direction. This concept is widely accepted in modern liberal democratic societies around the world, but you won't hear it on your news station. The belief is that the masses are too dumb and hysterical to manage and think for themselves, and need privileged (rich) and intellectual (smart) people to direct them and put them on the right path.

Back about a hundred years ago, there was a guy named Walter Lippmann, and he called the population the **bewildered herd**. He thought, like a lot of intellectuals then and now, that we have to protect ourselves from the rage and trampling of the bewildered herd. And he said you can do this by **the manufacture of consent**. That means you create people's opinions and agreement about those opinions through propaganda, so you don't need to force them to do something they may disagree with. If you control their minds through indoctrination and media propaganda, you don't have to control them violently (with the police). So, in the modern semi-free society, unlike the fascist regimes you see in old movies, propaganda is not in your face and out there like it used to be with scary posters and films.

This media framing of the debate, directed by society's owners, is how propaganda works in a semi-open society. If you want to be part of the mainstream, get a job, and have people like you, you don't talk about things outside of the framework others expect.

One way the public mind is controlled is through the corporate media system.

The corporate media system defines the rules of engagement for all people to talk about in certain areas. For example, it says there is a left and a right in political thought, that there is an eternal struggle between the two, and that the only discussion they will allow on their channels is between those two poles. Of course, this level of debate is very limited, but that is the point. There is a range of discussion that those who own our society (elites) want to allow us to have (things that benefit them and don't upset the apple cart). There are only specific acceptable topics we can discuss; anything outside those topics is inappropriate and will not be allowed on corporate media outlets. This is the permissible framework of debate.

Scholars like Noam Chomsky call this agenda-setting. The agenda and the framework surrounding it are created by the larger corporate media companies, which have the resources to control it (for example, only large media companies can send journalists overseas). The smaller local media outlets then follow that agenda and framework set by the large media companies, in part because they don't have the resources to send reporters on their own.

All those big media companies, FOX, CNN, MSNBC, are agenda-setting companies, and they care about profit, not truth, like any company that has a product to sell and a market to sell it to.

Chomsky discusses a tested hypothesis of his, the *Propaganda Model,* which, in essence, is what I described above in layman's terms. The hypothesis proposes that the media is not here to enlighten us, provide unbiased news, and keep the government in check, as they have claimed.

The corporate media's role is to create and enforce a propaganda framework that helps the rich keep the population under control and aligned with their goals and values.

The media accomplishes this by only focusing their reporting on specific issues and subjects (you know the list). They then present what both sides are saying within a limited framework, filtering out information unacceptable to their elite owners (e.g., not reporting on large protests). Finally, corporate media uses tone and emphasis to cast a distorted light on certain topics, aiming to sway them in one direction or the other.

Chomsky has a book and a movie called Manufacturing Consent, which presents his theory, backed by extensive research and scientific evidence, about how the media system in America really works, rather than what they tell us it does.

The story you have heard is that the media is here to provide a check on the government and to help people with information that enlightens and informs them. The actual model of the press is a mouthpiece for the elite establishment, presenting a positive image of the world that defends the economic, political, and social agendas of the elite groups that own society and run the economy.

AFTER the indoctrination, the reinforced conditioning, and the endless stream of propaganda and entertainment diversions being pumped into everyone day and night in every form of media, there are still some pesky people out there who will not get with the program and do what they are told and think what they are told to believe.

These people (Occupy Wall Street, BLM) aren't buying into the '*America is the greatest thing since sliced bread*' fantasy and see something is wrong here, and not at all what is being peddled in the media and from our business and political leaders. These disgruntled people go out and protest, write unpleasant blogs, and publish pamphlets (like this one) that question the script and storyline the elites have fed us for years. For these troublemakers, if the mind can't be controlled, there is one final option to control someone – physically.

The final stage of control is the POLICE.

The police in America are not being given military gear like assault rifles, bulletproof vests, noxious gas, and armored ATVs to protect citizens from terrorist or foreign threats, even though that was the initial justification for doing so. Anyone who is old enough to remember 9/11 may recall that right after it happened, police and military with assault rifles and body armor appeared on our streets protecting important places like train depots and ship ports. No one said a thing about it at the time, since to do so would not be supporting America against terrorism.

You will now see that those militarized police have never gone away. The powers-that-be, in fact, used that event as a rationale to expand their persecution and abuse of the populace with an increasing array of militarized equipment and responses. Domestic police in America are now indistinguishable from a military force and use their weapons of death against their own populace.

The police are being armed and trained this way to protect the rich and powerful against you, the individual. The police are employed to keep the status quo as is, and if any citizen is a threat to the status quo as defined by the elites, then the police, without qualms, will deal with that threat. In their eyes, it is their job.

YOU are the enemy the police are being armed for.

This process is well underway. First, as you see on the news, the militarized police have been used to quell racial violence and keep minorities in their ghettos (Ferguson, MO), where they are quarantined away from white wealth and privilege. Second, police were used to stomp out popular anti-corporate movements like Occupy Wall Street (mission successful!); and finally, they were deployed to stop peaceful demonstrations for any anti-government demonstration (arresting journalists at Trump's Inauguration). The use of police against peaceful protesters, political opponents, and dissenters in general will escalate in the coming years as the population continues to suffer due to economic hardships and rampant inequality.

YOU keep hearing me use the word 'propaganda,' so let's talk about what it means in a modern context and how it is used to control individuals and groups.

Propaganda is information that is created and disseminated to the public to try to change their opinion on something (Muslims are bad) or motivate them to a particular action (lock them up!). Propaganda is not information created with the intent to inform or educate. Its very purpose is to manipulate, not educate.

Propaganda will mix in some truth and facts to try to distort an issue to garner public support for something, let's say a war or a revolution. I described to you in some detail how elitist American revolutionaries gained support from the common man by using propaganda very effectively, convincing people who did not want to revolt to become revolutionaries by telling them their struggle was based on values like freedom and liberty and religious belief, not the greed and self-interest of the ruling class.

When you hear the word propaganda, you probably think back to World War 2 and those ridiculous posters of Germans telling you how bad the Jews were, or Americans telling you how evil the Japs were. That is old-school propaganda, which no longer exists except in places like North Korea. Modern propaganda has become much more refined and streamlined and is now fully integrated into the fabric of our society.

So, what does today's propaganda look like?

Support the Troops.

This is an excellent example of modern propaganda. First, the statement doesn't really mean anything. What is supporting the troops exactly? How do you do that specifically? Second, it is not a statement you can disagree with. Who doesn't support our troops? Anyone who disagrees with this is surely not a patriot.

This is propaganda. It has no real meaning, it can't be disagreed with, but it is put out there and made pervasive, and everyone rallies around it with bumper stickers, little signs, and ribbons. Good propaganda like this takes on a life of its own and self-perpetuates as people willingly spread it.

That is an obvious example. But most propaganda is unspoken and woven into our culture through our educational system (grades, competition), sports (winning, competition), movies and TV (being successful, stopping threats to freedom), and church (never question authority and do what you're told).

Who is putting out all this propaganda, and who benefits from spending billions of dollars each year on PR, partisan think tanks, advertising, and marketing to create, modify, and direct people's opinions?

Corporations, Churches, and the Government all benefit from people being subservient, compliant, and competitive.

We are all being molded and conditioned to be good little cogs in the great money-making machine that is the United States of America. In this system, each of us is either a consumer who buys goods and services, a worker who markets or sells goods or services, or a soldier who kills things so we can get cheaper goods and services. That is our function, and what the elites want us to be, and what they want our world to be. If you don't perform one of those functions, you are a deviant and potential criminal. But don't worry, there are lots of for-profit prisons out there, and using prisoners as slave labor is a great business model for elites. Get the undesirable out of the way and lock them up, then use them as cheap slave labor to make you more money. Then get the government to subsidize and fund you, and it is one hell of a profitable business model.

Ever wonder why the United States has the work culture it has? Because business leaders and owners in our society not only run businesses but also govern and shape society as a whole, they set the tone and conditions that all of us are bred into. Of course, they want us working 12+ hour days, 6-7 days a week, for starvation wages. It benefits business owners quite well, who can move those productivity gains into their own bank accounts, buy jets and boats, and eventually leave all that money to their kids to extend their family dynasty beyond their own lives (The Rockefellers).

LANGUAGE, or the words we use and don't use, is a key element for creating and maintaining a framework of propaganda that keeps social conversations and ideas in line with what the rich want you to talk and think about. In general, the boundaries and rules of political debate are designed to prevent free and independent thought. You must have a conversation within the limits of what the ruling class or their representatives (corporate media, elite university professors, politicians, CEOs) want you to have. They do this by denying you the words or the linguistic framework that would allow you to have a meaningful discussion.

There are several methods for accomplishing this limitation to free speech and free thought. First, certain words are used that have loaded or dual meanings, so that just using those words limits you to certain assumptions you may disagree with initially. In the case of dual-meaning words, there is what the word literally means, and then there is the secret meaning it implies, unspoken.

Let's use the word *terrorism* as an example. This is an important word because, since the end of the Cold War, it has been used to justify much of our military spending and the reduction of civil liberties and individual rights. You will notice that terrorism is only something other people and countries do. Even though, by definition, America as a state engages in and supports terrorist activity all over the world. You will also notice that terrorism only applies to brown people from different religions (Islam). When a white Christian shoots up a Planned Parenthood or blows up a Jewish church, it meets all the definitions of a terrorist act. Yet, the Justice Department and FBI do not classify any white American engaged in terrorist activities as a terrorist, unless, of course, they joined ISIS or became a Muslim, then they can be a terrorist.

Democracy is another loaded, dual-meaning term. You will notice across the world that what America calls a democracy is simply a country that agrees with us and follows our direction on the world stage. Any country that disagrees and doesn't line up with what we want, we call them socialist, communist, or something other than a democracy. In other countries, anyone who follows our orders and does what they are told is a moderate, and anyone who doesn't is a radical, whether they are left or right.

Another dual-meaning code word is *entitlements*. That is code for the social services that regular people get (healthcare, unemployment, Social Security) that the rich don't think they deserve. But when the government gives the same taxpayer money to businesses and the rich, they call it subsidies, not entitlements, or, even better, call it defense and funnel the money to private tech R&D through the Pentagon as research (DARPA).

Another loaded word is *defense*. Have you ever noticed that everything America does on the world stage is defense? We only defend ourselves against the spread of tyranny, to support democracy and freedom, and to stop others from somehow impacting our way of life. This strategy to call all military action defensive was established from day one in the US with the Mexican War and continues through self-manufactured events to trigger defensive wars like the Spanish-American War (Remember the Maine) and the Iraq War (WMDs).

PROPAGANDA works best when no one knows that it is propaganda. If you put it in history books and have respectable teachers teach it to kids, then it's history and fact. Put it in enough books, tell the story enough times, and it all becomes real and unchallengeable.

I want to use **The Discovery of America** as a prime example of history as propaganda, and how dramatic historical storytelling can help to create a framework of characters, with heroes and villains, to make the story more believable for young people. You heard me before challenge the assumption that the United States of America created a better life for the majority of the people in it, that it, in fact benefitted the new American elites more than anyone else, and helped to propel a new set of social owners over the masses whom overall did not see an improvement in their lives due to the American Revolution.

But what is the USA if not a beacon of democracy and freedom, as the history books tell you? What is it if it's not a grand experiment of enlightened men?

The United States of America is, and always has been, a business enterprise.

Its goal, which is not coincidentally the end goal of our country's owners, implemented through the apparatus of the state (laws, courts, police, politicians), is to use its citizens as resources to fuel and fund a generational transfer scheme in which wealth is siphoned out of the poorer and middle classes into the pockets of the rich.

From day one, the people who discovered and opened the New World to resource exploitation were paid to go there and do just that. Columbus and his ilk were not great explorers of an age gone by, but rather contract labor for merchant investors to go to new places, find resources (gold, silver, spices, fur, slaves), and bring them back home for a tidy profit.

I want to present Christopher Columbus and the Discovery of America as a prime example of how the narrative of our discovery and founding was manufactured to meet certain public relations and political goals, resulting in a new national narrative that has become enshrined as historical fact.

In the 19th century, there was a huge trend in historical fiction, as many major writers created fictionalized versions of historical figures and events to sell nostalgia (remember when things were better and simpler) and promote patriotic feelings (USA! USA!). Much of the modern American history taught in schools is derived from these fictionalized accounts of the 1800s written by fictional writers.

One of the books that started this craze was *A History of the Life and Voyages of Christopher Columbus* by Washington Irving. Irving was a fiction writer, not a historian or biographer, and he created a fictionalized version of Columbus's persona and biography to foster a patriotic myth about the founding of America. He wrote a book that was part fact and part fiction. The trouble is, these two things can get mixed up, and people lose which is which over time. The book Irving wrote about Columbus is not a historical biography, yet it has been treated as such, becoming enshrined as fact and taught in our schools.

Before the 19th century, no one in this country had even heard of Christopher Columbus. Back then, it wasn't just blacks who were persecuted; bigoted people in America didn't much like Irish or Italian immigrants either. Italian leaders of the time were looking for a way to create some good PR for the Italian immigrants, who were being harshly treated and racially persecuted in the United States. So, the pro-Italian public relations campaign used the Irving book as its foundation to promote Italian-Americans as decent and productive people.

With this book and subsequent PR campaign, the Columbus myth and narrative were created, promoted, and disseminated into the American mainstream. Eventually, it was written into history books and taught to children as a historical fact. The fictional story we all know was that Columbus discovered America (he did not), that he was a great explorer and visionary (he was an incompetent charlatan who lied about what he found to his investors), and that he opened up to the civilized world an uninhabited New World ripe for exploitation (millions of people already inhabited it).

To give you an idea of who Columbus really was as a person, this is a direct quote from him in his personal log on meeting Native Americans for the first time on the island we now call Haiti –

"With fifty men, we could subjugate them all and make them do whatever we want."

From the first days of Columbus, gold wasn't the only resource the Spanish were interested in. The other resource was slaves. Since indigenous people in those days were not considered human, but commonly referred to as savages, they, like animals, had no rights and could be bought and sold like horses or other barnyard commodities.

In 1495, Columbus set up a base in Haiti. Since he was not able to find gold to bring home to his benefactors as he promised, Columbus rounded up local people to be sold as slaves to try to salvage the expedition and make a profit. He picked 500 native slaves to ship back to Spain to sell. Two hundred died en route. It was not a very profitable affair.

Since Columbus wasn't bringing back enough gold and too many slaves died en route to make his benefactors happy with their investment, he stepped up the pressure on the locals to produce what he needed to satisfy them – more gold. On Columbus's orders, Native Americans in Haiti were told to bring a certain amount of gold to the Spaniards every three months; if they got some, they were given a copper token to hang around their necks as proof. Any Native American who didn't have a copper token around their neck had their hands cut off. The ultimatum from Columbus was simple: either give us gold, or we'll kill you. Since there wasn't any substantial gold in Haiti for the natives to turn in, they ran and were hunted down with dogs and killed.

Eventually, in light of the cruelty, superior weapons, and technology the Spanish had, the Native Americans began mass suicides, poisoning their own children to save them from Spanish cruelty and slavery. In only two years, through murder or suicide, it is estimated that half of the 250,000 Native Americans in Haiti were dead.

After it was clear no more gold was to be found in Haiti, the Indians were worked to death in forced labor camps, and by 1550, there were only 500 Native Americans (Arawak) left on the island. By 1650, they were eliminated through genocide. In a little more than 150 years, the first Native Americans who encountered Europeans were massacred.

After Columbus and his genocide of the Arawak people, a similar pattern was followed as Cortés did the same thing to the Aztecs in Mexico, Pizarro to the Incas of Peru, and the English settlers of Virginia and Massachusetts did to the Powhatans and Pequot Native Americans.

Up north on the mainland, the Native Americans were more challenging to control than those in Haiti. They had more numbers than the English invaders, knew the land better, and could track and hunt more effectively. Hence, the invaders needed more indirect and deceptive methods to control the native population. Since they could not fight the Native Americans directly in battle, they decided to resort to deception and massacres of women and children to achieve victory.

This strategy to attack non-combatants to cause terror and capitulation was the primary strategy used by Cortés and the English to subdue Native Americans in the formation of America.

From the first confrontations with indigenous Americans, the European invaders and aggressors claimed they were attacked and were defending their lives. This rationale will be repeated time and time through American history to justify aggressive acts and declarations of war (The Mexican War, The Spanish-American War, The Iraq War).

No one today knows the exact number of people living in North and South America before the Spanish- and English-led invasions. Still, it is estimated that north of Mexico, the Indian population of 10 million would be reduced to fewer than 1 million. Granted, many of those native people were lost to disease (smallpox) that was brought over by the European settlers, but keep in mind the goal of the settlers was to subjugate or eliminate the native population. Hence, the diseases that wiped them out just expedited what deliberately happened to the remaining indigenous population. By 1820, only 120,000 Indians still lived east of the Mississippi. By 1844, fewer than 30,000 were left. The majority of them were forced to migrate westward on an extended death march. (Trail of Tears).

This is the beginning of history in the New World, a history defined by cruelty, slavery, profit, violence, and death. A beginning that is barely mentioned in the history books that have indoctrinated American youth for the past several hundred years.

The story of the discovery of America is an excellent example of history as propaganda and a fictionalized narrative. America was invaded, not discovered. America was not unpopulated; millions of people were already living here. Those millions of people were enslaved, murdered, and forced into labor and subservience to enrich the opportunists who came here looking for wealth and profit.

The invasion of the New World was the beginning of the modern system of economy, power, and control that has dominated the world for the last 500 years.

In the end, did the invasion of the New World really lead to a better life for the human population overall? For Spain, all the gold, silver, and slaves they took did not make the Spanish people any better off. Their current rulers used the wealth to gain a temporary edge in power and to hire more soldiers to fight in their wars. In the end, though, the rulers of Spain lost those wars, and some other elite families in different countries took control, and then lost control, over and over, generation to generation.

Has anything really changed for the rest of us?

I'D like to present a final example of history as propaganda. We have all been told throughout our lives how the Civil War was a moral battle in the United States, and that the Northerners were against slavery. The South was for slavery, and Abraham Lincoln was a great, forward-looking Renaissance man who freed the slaves, united the country, and made all Americans equal.

This is, of course, pure propaganda and not accurate at all. Still, after it was repeated millions of times and published in history books for all ages, it has become fact and a national narrative intended to give Americans the illusion that they live in a society of justice, freedom, and equality.

Let's look at what slavery was really all about, why the Civil War happened, and how Abraham Lincoln's real feelings about blacks play into our actual national history, not the propagandized narrative that has been spoon-fed to us as children.

You heard before about how the Spanish and others who came to the Caribbean first enslaved and abused the natives to profit from them. Well, it turned out that when the English and others landed in North Virginia and whatnot, the locals there were far too numerous and not so easy to control or enslave for the invaders' benefit. When those northern Indians in the Americas couldn't be managed and enslaved by the next wave of pioneers, slaves from Africa were shipped in to get the job done.

As a side note, when discussing the slave trade, we are talking about Europeans as a group that drove and developed the modern trade of human beings. It was a full 50 years before Columbus that the Portuguese took 10 African blacks to Lisbon, starting the modern regular trade of black slaves. In the Americas, by the year 1619, 1 million blacks had already been brought from Africa to South America and the Caribbean to work in Portuguese and Spanish colonies as slaves before they ever set foot in Jamestown. By 1800, 10 to 15 million blacks had been transported to America as slaves.

It is estimated that Africa lost **50 million people** to death and slavery at the beginning of modern Western civilization.

The race war in America between whites and blacks, which continues today, was a deliberate system of social and physical controls and taboos that were designed to reinforce the system of slavery and economic repression against the millions of Africans who were kidnapped and forced into subservience. Slave control was accomplished by paying poor whites to be the overseers of black labor and be the buffer for black hatred against wealthy white elites.

After the end of the slave trade, the federal government was as guilty as anyone for perpetuating African Americans' repressive situation. They weakly enforced the laws that ended the slave trade, but enforced the laws when returning fugitives to slavery. The federal government collaborated with the South to keep abolitionist literature out of the states.

To give you an idea of how educated white people in the North viewed black people in the 19th century, I present this quote from Abraham Lincoln, the Great Emancipator, just before his election.

"I will say, then, that I am not, nor ever have been, in favor of bringing about in any way the social and political equality of white and black races (applause); that I am not, nor ever have been, in favor of making voters or jurors of negroes, nor of qualifying them to hold office, not to intermarry with white people…And inasmuch as they cannot so live, while they do remain together there must be the position of superior and inferior, and I as much as any other man am in favor or having the superior position assigned to the white race."

I present to you Abraham Lincoln – The White Supremacist.

The US Civil War was not about slavery as a moral institution, as is claimed and advertised. Most northerners didn't care enough about slavery to put their necks on the line for it in an actual war. Lincoln's white supremacist worldview was mainstream thought at the time for educated liberal northerners like Lincoln.

The Civil War, just like the Revolution before it, was a battle of elites jockeying for power and control.

The northern elites wanted economic expansion in a developing, industrializing economy, including free labor, free land, a free market, high tariffs on manufacturers in the South, and a federal, centralized bank. Elites who ran plantations in the South had a slave-based feudal system and wanted nothing of modern industrialization (unless they were in charge), and saw their way of life being threatened and their position as owners of their society being usurped by rival elites.

This quote is from Lincoln's first inaugural address.

"I have no purpose, directly or indirectly, to interfere with the institution of slavery in the States where it exists. I believe I have no lawful right to do so, and I have no inclination to do so."

It was not until the Civil War was growing uglier and grimmer, with many casualties on both sides, and as Lincoln was losing the support of abolitionists (anti-slave people), that he was forced to act on slavery and become the Great Emancipator to maintain power and control.

In one of Lincoln's private letters to a general, you get a true understanding of the man's feelings about blacks and slavery.

"My paramount object in this struggle is to save the Union, and is not either to save or destroy slavery. If I could save the Union without freeing any slave, I would do it; and if I could save it by freeing all the slaves, I would do it; and if I could do it by freeing some and leaving others alone, I would also do that."

Abraham Lincoln made the Civil War about slavery as a political tool to win the war and establish the northern elites as the new ruling class of America.

The story of the Civil War is historical propaganda. It was not a battle between good and evil, for slavery and freedom, for liberty and justice. It was a **war of greed and control,** like all others. It was a war of elites, as they fought for control of the Union and for their way of life to be imposed on other elites and their minions (Industrialization vs. Feudalism). Everyone else was just cannon fodder for this elite power struggle.

And if you think things went well for slaves after Abraham Lincoln came down off his white supremacy high horse to emancipate them, he and the federal government pretty much left them to their own devices to be used and abused by their former southern masters for the next century until the people partially freed themselves in the Civil Rights movement of the 1960s.

Here is a quote from a former slave named Tomas Hall about what happened to them after Lincoln took the credit for their freedom.

"Lincoln got the praise for freeing us, but did he do it? He gave us freedom without giving us any chance to live to ourselves and we still had to depend on the southern white man for work, food, and clothing, and he held us out of necessity and want in a state of servitude but little better than slavery. "

Were the slaves really freed, or were they just put into another kind of bondage and control, one a little opaque than and not as direct as outright slavery? Their physical slavery quickly turned into wage slavery through various social and economic controls for the next century.

I give you these two important historical examples to show just how big and brazen propaganda is. It is written into the very fabric of our known world and is programmed into us as children as a fact we never once consider challenging, our entire lives. The Civil War was about slavery, and America was founded by Columbus, just as it is assumed that the sky is blue and the sun will rise every day.

THE indoctrination and conditioning meant to mold you into compliant behavior, the potential threat of the police if you don't cower to the elites, as well as endless distractions for the population like sports, alcohol, and entertainment, don't completely insulate those in charge from the fury of the populace if they get too greedy or out of line themselves.

To counter this, throughout modern human history, the elite have cloaked themselves in mystery and code to make themselves appear untouchable and unknowable to the common man. Those in power want you to think they occupy a special place as humans, distinct from the lowly citizen. They want you to think they have something special in their DNA, some unique abilities, or a privileged upbringing that makes them the appropriate designees of power. Only they can be trusted to make important decisions for the rest of us.

Those in charge feel they deserve to be where they are, just like all rich people believe they deserve their wealth, regardless of how they got it.

It's ironic how the rich talk despairingly about entitlements for the general population (social security, healthcare), while they themselves are the most entitled of all social strata (tax breaks, subsidies). They firmly believe in their greatness, their superiority, and their entitlement to control all the money and power.

This cloak of mystery surrounding power has been in place since the first human societies developed thousands of years ago. Remember when I talked about how families maintain power across generations by shaping social structure, controlling communication, and shaping the telling of historical events? Well, their activities are enabled and shielded by a cloak of mystery and code that surrounds their power.

Royalty, the family dynasties that run monarchies, systems where they were in absolute control, claiming to be either Gods themselves or descendants of Gods, are a classic example of how this method was implemented successfully to control the populace for millennia. The concept of royalty, called the Divine Right of Kings, creates a special class of people in society, someone beyond standard conventions and norms, whom regular people could not possibly understand or ever be like. Before people knew better thanks to science, royal people were believed to be either divinely (by God) descended or appointed and approved. Now, in most countries, they are a quaint reminder of tradition, but their rule over humanity was cruel, elitist, and completely lacking in the consent of the people they governed.

Aside from the obvious religious implication, why would the ordinary person buy into this deal, so obviously on the losing end of being managed by a superior group of people who look down on everyone else? The reason is broadcast daily from corporate media and from every nook and cranny of the establishment. And that reason has been used to motivate and influence people since the dawn of civilization.

You, the individual, must be aware that there are horrific threats and enemies (communists, Islamic terrorists, Jews, drug addicts, blacks, liberals, immigrants) about to destroy us at all times, from within and without. To protect ourselves, we must grant some elite who are smarter and wiser than we are the authority to protect us from imminent destruction.

All governments use FEAR to control the populace, and the need for mystery and secrecy is a core element of it.

Government, just like royalty and all forms of power, shrouds itself in a cloak of mystery and code to shield itself from accountability and visibility. You can't criticize something you can't see or even know about. For this reason, the government applies everything it does under a cloak of secrecy, as it puts all its internal communication and policy decisions behind classified documents status to keep the public in the dark about its true motivations and activities.

Overwhelmingly, the primary purpose of government secrecy is not to protect information from foreign adversaries but to keep information from the view of the American public to avoid accountability and oversight.

The purpose of government secrecy is to marginalize the population.

AS you heard me mention earlier, the idea that you have free will and are an independent being is an illusion. As a concept, free will is promoted and leveraged by those in charge to control and manipulate you, directing you where they want you to be. If you are programmed with certain assumptions as an infant and small child, you never question the foundational programming that determines many of your life choices and path. You can never get out of line since you are only going to operate in the framework you think exists.

Imagine you are a rat in a maze. You run around the maze, and it seems you have the option to turn in whatever direction you want to follow whatever path you want. You go left, right, and then left again, and in the end, you get a small piece of cheese. Looking at it from the rat's perspective, he has total free will. He goes where he wants, when he wants, and gets rewarded for it. The rat has a limited perspective and limited access to the maze he lives in, but from his individual perspective, he is in complete control and free to go where he wants.

You, as a human, are in the same situation as the rat. Depending on where you were born and who you become, you only have access to a part of the maze. If you were born poor, you have minimal access and can only move in a few scripted directions. If you were born to an upper-middle-class business person, you have access to more of the maze than the poor person, but are still limited by those above you. If you are a part of the millionaire lackey elite, you have access to most of the maze but still have to operate within approved boundaries by the owners/maze managers. Finally, if you are a true elite and a real owner of society, like a billionaire or a King, you not only have a complete run of the maze but can also change the maze's structure to grant special access and benefits for you and your friends.

Our life is a script, one that has been programmed into us to turn us into commodities for the business machine called The United States of America. We are only of use to the machine as long as we fulfill our prescribed role.

THE illusion of choice is key to supporting and enforcing the illusion of free will. Like the rat, you are given prescribed options as a voter and consumer to make you feel like you have choices. Just like a rat turning left and right in a maze as many times as you like, you, the individual, also have the same illusion of perspective.

Every few years, you get to choose between left and right in an election and are told that this choice is critical to you being a free and independent person in a democracy. You are also told that if you don't choose one or the other, then it's your fault if things don't go well. You had the choice to vote, and you didn't, so the accountability lies with you for our problems, not with our leaders, since we are in a democracy and the people make all the decisions. The leaders are just servants to the people.

Part of the whole myth of the United States is that it is a representative democracy, a new form of forward-looking government that is of the people, by the people, and for the people. There are intermediaries called congressmen and the like that represent you, since you, the dumb herd animal, can't possibly make democratic decisions on your own. Luckily, there are smart and well-born elites who run things for you, and let you know what jobs you can have, how much money you are allowed to make, what policies you will vote for, and what issues you should care about.

So, while the United States claims to be a representative democracy and has all the structure and form of one, it does not function like a real democracy (direct or representative). If it did, it would mean the populace had democratic input into major decisions and planning, such as setting policy and allocating capital investment. All of this is carried out outside the public and democratic sphere, solely by the elites and their representatives. The populace participates only in corporate, elite-approved discussions and debates, limited by the media outlets and the framework they establish.

This whole infrastructure and code surrounding it is all to give you, the individual, the public, the illusion of free will and choice. The elites want you to think you are in a democracy and make decisions about things. It's like when you let your kids win a game, knowing you could beat them whenever you want.

Elites are humoring you with the spectacle of democracy.

You will see, time and time again, that when anything threatens the actual power structure, the illusion of democracy is quickly dispelled (2000 U.S. Presidential Election, 2016 Democratic Primaries). You'll also see that when one of the elite's henchmen lackeys gets out of line and threatens the true power structure, they will be taken out of position and replaced (Nixon).

Looking at it from a strict definition point of view, America could more appropriately be called a Plutocracy or Plutarchy. (A plutocratic oligarchy), which is a government run by a small group of the rich and powerful, for the benefit of the rich and powerful. You could call the U.S. a lot of other things, like a Corporatocracy, a Kleptocracy, or a Patriarchy. But the one thing I would not call the U.S. is a democracy.

Does this sound closer to the America that was described in this pamphlet?

Let's talk a little more about how the illusion of choice is used to give you, the individual, the impression that you live in a democratic society.

America is not the two-party system people have commonly claimed it is. This is embedded propaganda from birth to present, an illusion of choice and inclusion to the general population. I am right or left, and I belong to one group, and the other group is terrible and immoral and the exact opposite of what we believe. This is the way members of both parties are conditioned and reinforced to think.

The United States of America has a one-party system with two factions.

That party is the pro-business party, and both factions agree on and align with all its pro-business policies. Watch for which bills get passed when the warring parties can't agree on anything. It's always military funding (Pentagon research subsidies), budget increases, and pro-business policies; they always have universal support. It's all the fluff around it that all conversation and debate is directed to publicly (abortion) that deflects from the true nature and allegiances of all the pro-business politicians who are all bought and paid for by similar corporate interests.

The pro-business party has a far-right faction (The GOP) and a centrist-right faction (The Democrats). Even though there are only two major factions within the same party, there are many more subgroups of elites in our country that dispute one another and fight over power and control, shifting ownership back and forth in a never-ending tug-of-war for advantage and position. Does this sound a little like how elite families maintain power over generations? Not surprising to see that same process happening in the apparatus of the state (politics), which is just a servant to those really in control (the ultra-rich).

The illusion of choice isn't just about voting and pseudo-democracies; it is used to give people the illusion of choice when it comes to products, goods, and services as well. If you looked out at the business world and saw all the products and brands out there, you would say there are tremendous choices and options for consumers to buy whatever they want from lots of different companies. Just like in the illusion of the two-party system, the number of businesses and brands is an illusion, meant to give you the impression of choice.

For example, only 10 companies control the vast majority of large food and beverage brands worldwide. In the corporate media space, only about six companies control nearly all the news and information we hear and see. But way back in the early 80s, before Bill Clinton deregulated telecommunications, the media was divided into over 50 companies.

Do you think this consolidation of media by wealthy corporate owners could be affecting our ability to access free, independent news and information? If we had a true democracy, how could it function without access to reliable and authentic news and information?

EARLIER you heard me talk about monarchies, systems of family rule that derived their power by claiming to either be Gods themselves, the descendants of God, or were directly appointed by God to rule all of humanity below them. These systems worked for thousands of years across the whole world and allowed a tiny group of elites to run society mostly unchallenged by the rank and file.

These family monarchies use/used religion (Christianity, Islam) as a tool to control the population. Eventually, religion became so intertwined with government and power that they merged into a single institution. For this pamphlet, let's call it the Church-State. This is a society in which the church's goals and objectives are indistinguishable from the apparatus of the state. For example, back in England, before they had their own revolution, you were required by law to attend church, their church, every Sunday. If you didn't, you could be fined or imprisoned. You were forced through the framework of the state (legislation, courts, police) to adhere to the beliefs and opinions (and power structure) of the church. This still goes on in many Islamic states today.

When the last wave of worldwide revolutions happened in the 18th and 19th centuries, the common man revolted against this system of church and state, feeling that power should be derived from the consent of the people to be governed in some democratic fashion. It didn't take long after many countries revolted that they became dictatorships (France) or a fusion of business and state (The United States of America). We will call this the Corporate State. This is a society in which business corporations manage and plan the economic and social infrastructure for the benefit of corporations and their owners.

Their owners, the corporate power elite, set the policies that their corporate organizations implement and the rest of us have to operate within. They directly influence politicians with lots of money, through political groups, and solely set the framework for debate. The populace has almost no role in what our representatives discuss or where they decide to invest for our country's growth and future.

The government of the corporate state will put its resources behind advancing business interests, while simply not supporting the general populace in terms of enforcement or planning. The population in the corporate state is a commodity. You have no value more than any other commodity a company owns. Whether it is real estate, paper, computers, or intellectual property, you can be disposed of with no afterthought if you no longer have value to the corporate profit system.

To give you some idea of how extensively this level of corporatism has infected our country over the last few centuries, in the United States, corporations have been legally treated as individuals since the mid-19th century and have almost all the rights a person can have.

How can non-existent entities that have no form beyond what a human gives them be legally thought of as people themselves? How can they be considered people if they cannot be held personally accountable for illegal actions? In America, corporations are considered by law to be eternal people who can own land and assets but can't be held responsible for any crime.

Please go check out the documentary *The Corporation* for more background on corporations and how they came to take over our government and way of life. The corporate state is run solely by corporate interests for corporate gain. The public is sidelined until public opinion becomes significant enough to cause some level of capitulation and sway, typically financial.

Public opinion is the one weapon people still have to exercise some influence on politicians and corporations. The elite are scared of people getting together and causing problems for them. It could be bad PR, property damage, unpleasant new stories, significant strikes, or consumer boycotts. The corporate state will try to keep public opinion in line by using propaganda and a few scraps of contrition. Still, if the general population starts acting up too much, the police can easily be marshaled to crack some skulls and break up protests.

Until people come to terms and start to discuss the corporate state and the corporatocracy we currently live in, nothing that the institution is causing (global warming, wars, poverty, and economic inequality) will be dealt with. The goal of power and control is to keep this conversation from happening. They will do everything they can to divert the discussion away from real cause and effect and try to direct it to subjects and topics they find beneficial or less harmful to their interests. The elite use their domination of corporate media outlets to push their corporatist viewpoints to the public to downplay and diminish the influence of corporations on our lives and our pseudo-democracy.

CONCLUSION

THIS pamphlet was written for one purpose. To help illustrate to you, the individual, how certain people (really rich ones) manipulate and control you so you will act in a way that is beneficial to them. Elites have been doing this type of control and manipulation for millennia. The devices they use now are more advanced and transparent, but the structure of power and control remains the same as it did 3,000 years ago. If you learn to spot these controls under the surface of what is presented to you, you will be more able to defend yourself against manipulation.

The goal of this pamphlet is to allow you, the inhabitants of America, to live a freer and more authentic life by possessing alternate information that those in charge have decided not to provide to you.

We started by discussing how the American Revolution was not a war of liberty and popular revolt as it was presented in history class, but rather a struggle for elite control over society and its resources. New elites in America wanted to take control from older elites in England and manufactured a revolution to elevate them to the position of ownership in our society. The new American elites used propaganda in the form of the Declaration of Independence, the US Constitution, and pamphlets like Common Sense to buy support from underlings that would become the middle class, and to convince the poor that they would be fighting for God, liberty, freedom, and justice – instead of just switching one rich master for another.

We then talked about how control is applied and maintained over generations through interconnected systems of social indoctrination (parents, school, church, leaders), an ongoing process of reinforced conditioning of that indoctrination (media, lower and higher education, work, sports), institutionalized systems built to pit one group of people against another (racism, sexism, politics), and finally physical controls in case anyone gets out of line with their indoctrination and conditioning (police, courts, jail, execution). These control systems are bolstered by a few key tactics used concurrently to support them and provide rationale and cover for their activities.

The use and evolution of propaganda have been a key element to the success of the modern system of social control that started during the invasion of the New World. In modern semi-open societies like ours, old-school military violence against the populace is typically more of a last resort, while controlling people with more indirect and subconscious methods is more effective at maintaining control over long periods of time across many economic groups.

Our very language is loaded and used in ways that limit our ability to have authentic, free-thinking discussions. We lose before the game even starts because someone else wrote the rulebook and created a playing field we couldn't possibly win on. Words themselves lock us into a pre-approved conversation intended to produce no level of authentic discussion or results.

In addition to limitations on words and language, elites shroud themselves and their actions in veils of mystery and code, as if putting all internal government communications marked as classified, to make ordinary people think those in charge have a special mandate or ability to operate in a mysterious world.

All of this control and manipulation is made possible by presenting the individual and the population at large with the twin illusions of free will and free choice. All humans have an intrinsic need for freedom, inclusion, and meaning. By manipulating these intrinsic needs, by making people think they are freer than they are, by making people believe they are more included than they are, and by making people think they are participating in society more than they actually are, elites can give all strata of society the illusion of free will and choice over their collective direction.

All those decisions are made outside of your view and influenced by people who have appointed themselves as the leaders of our society, and who use the resources and infrastructure of society to further their own interests. This illusion of choice gives you the false impression that we live in an open democracy, that there are myriad opposing viewpoints in this society, and that you have an active role, since, once every few years, you can vote for one of two factions of the same ruling-class party.

In America, we have the pageantry and form of democracy without a true functioning democracy.

This illusion of choice has allowed the corporate state to take over all aspects of our society and government fully. Through relentless corporate lobbying, corruption, and PR, the corporate state now owns all major politicians from the single pro-business party, whether they belong to the GOP faction or the Democrat faction, and its elite owners set policy, plan capital investment, and do overall social and financial planning entirely outside the democratic process. The corporate state has presented the public with the illusion of multiple brands and companies, making them think there is far more diversity and competition than there actually is.

All these strategies and tactics, in which I use modern examples and historical precedent to help illuminate to you, the individual, how those with power can use them to control not just you, but society as a whole, for the benefit of the elite classes to the detriment of the rest.

The abuse and misuse of the majority by the elite minority is the real struggle in human history – and it continues to this day unabated.

This is a pamphlet of common sense, and it is addressed to the inhabitants of America, every single one of them.